T0156699

# WAR OF WORDS: HITLER'S DIPLOMATIC BLITZKRIEG

## A DIPLOMATIC VIEW FROM THE EAGLE'S NEST

DOUGLAS MOSSMAN

IUNIVERSE, INC.
NEW YORK  BLOOMINGTON

War of Words: Hitler's Diplomatic Blitzkrieg
A Diplomatic View from the Eagle's Nest

iUniverse books may be ordered through booksellers or by contacting:

iUniverse
1663 Liberty Drive
Bloomington, IN 47403
www.iuniverse.com
1-800-Authors (1-800-288-4677)

ISBN: 978-1-4401-8132-0 (sc)
ISBN: 978-1-4401-8133-7 (dj)
ISBN: 978-1-4401-8134-4 (ebk)

Printed in the United States of America

iUniverse rev. date: 7/5/2010

# TABLE OF CONTENTS

# I. ELEVATOR TALK

**Obersalzberg, Germany. The Eagle's Nest. August 1939.**

On a cool summer evening in August of 1939 near the peak of the Kehlstein Mountain a group of smartly dressed high ranking Nazis stepped from a fleet of 770 Mercedes Benzes to enter a tunnel bore through solid rock. The group, all cabinet members of the Third Reich strolled through the cold tunnel leading to a round antechamber where a brass and gold elevator cabin waited. They did not descend into a bunker but rather ascended up to the Kehlstein peak which bordered Germany and Austria. On the way up the architect Albert Speer glanced at his boss who seemed to be talking to himself: "I'll send Goring, or if need be I'll go myself," as if alluding to some yet unmentioned international meeting. The silence would not be broken again until the cabin arrived in a vestibule of the pavilion called, *D-Haus,* 6,000 ft above sea level.

※

The *D-Haus*, an acronym for "diplomats' house," is a spectacular hexagon shaped marble and granite structure built for the purpose of allowing the top Nazi to call secret meetings and conferences whenever he wished to do so.

From every window superb alpine mountain vistas are silhouetted against the sky, villages dot the landscape and occasionally a cloud floats by the window. Inside the large conference room, or the Great Hall, groupings of tables and chairs could accommodate gatherings of 100, off to the side is a descending staircase leading to a smaller den where a sofa and table becomes a comfortable space for just a few. Appointments are sparse but well placed, heavy oak furniture and big down pillow chairs rest on oriental rugs, and on the walls are hand-made tapestries and gold leaf candelabra sconces. Near the back of the building is the "Fuhrer Arbeitzimmer," or *Fuhrer study* for its owner. Finally, a long dining room could hold a formal dinner for 32. A kitchen and security personnel room completes the structure.

The first foreign diplomat to visit Hitler at the pavilion, French Amb. Francois Poncet referred to the house as the "Eagle's Nest" in his correspondences. The idea and realization of the structure was that of Reichsleiter (Reich leader) Martin Bormann, who was tasked by Rudolf Hess to oversee the construction of the Obersalzberg area where the Fuhrer had his private residence, Der Berghof. Bormann relished the responsibility and went on a spending spree, building for his Fuhrer a private green house, movie theater, a hotel for his guests, an archive for films and documents, a post office and an alpine chalet for business meetings. But the Eagle's Nest was the crown jewel of the Obersalzberg and the most expensive structure to build. The Obersalzberg security chief, SS Obersturmbannführer Bernhard Frank recalled that "Hitler could escape into the clouds to the Eagle's Nest where he could relax and entertain dignitaries and heads-of-state, to get away from the day to day chore of running a government."[2]

The Eagle's Nest became available to Hitler at a time when the Munich Agreement was behind him. By 1938 the Fuhrer had in his Nazi sphere of influence three million new German nationals from Czechoslovakia; he had annexed Austria and had taken back the Rhineland; and yet his appetite for more Lebensraum (living space) was still unfulfilled. At this time the international press enjoyed covering Hitler's exploits and as a result he soon became the news-reel star of the day. Hitler even allowed the international press to take pictures of his private residence, The Berghof and to circulate the pictures.

The down side was that the press was becoming increasingly critical of his internal polices as well as his aggressive foreign policy. The western democracies, in particular the Roosevelt administration were not taken in by Hitler's charisma and avoided Hitler at all costs. In fact President Roosevelt recalled the American ambassador in 1939 to protest Hitler's regime and its antics. Shortly thereafter the president made a last diplomatic effort to foil Hitler's aggression by sending Under Secretary of State Sumner Welles to Berlin, but this had little impact.

As a result of the growing animosity Hitler felt towards him and coupled with his growing weariness of the foreign press, "its ridicules me" he told foreign guests, Hitler realized he could avoid the press by having meetings at his new Eagle's Nest where it would be impossible for the press to "wait outside the front door" to resentfully announce that the Fuhrer committed another strong armed diplomatic blitz to get his way. Besides, the Eagle's Nest was up a privately secured four mile road. To confuse the press further journalist would be told in Berlin and in Munich that Der Fuhrer was relaxing at the Berghof, in fact Hitler would be waiting in the Eagle's Nest for dignitaries to be driven from the nearby Salzburg airport for a secret conference.

Back on that cold August evening in 1939 when Hitler and his inner circle looked forward to some rest and relaxation at the Eagle's Nest, he was cognizant of German folklore that professed King Charlemagne and his legendary armies slept in the caves of the Unterberg mountains across from the Kehlstein, to be awaken at the right moment to conquer the world.

It was in this atmosphere that Hitler was struck with the idea to weave a diplomatic blanket with Stalin to cloak his underlying military aspiration to divide Poland between them. Three weeks after this elevator ride, on August 23, 1939, Speer was again with Hitler, actually having dinner with him at the Berghof when a phone was handed to Hitler. Hitler slammed his fist onto the dinner table and exclaimed "I have them." Champagne was served. *"The Molotov–Ribbentrop Pact"* was signed. This allowed Hitler to invade Poland without Stalin's interference. World War II began the next week.

This is an untold story of frontline diplomacy, told through the voices and recollections of those who met with Hitler between mid-September 1938 and October 1940 in the Eagle's Nest. These diplomats and officials from France, Italy and League of Nations did not ask to meet the Fuhrer, but rather it was Nazidom's default lead diplomat, the Fuhrer who begged their attendance to hear his needs for geopolitical entitlements.

The dialogue, descriptions of place and photographs within are taken from captured Nazi records, Hitler' and Eva Braun's photo albums and from the memoirs of those who met with Hitler and witnesses who were in the Eagle's Nest at that time. These critical negotiations on the eve of World War II have all but been overlooked by historians.

This study ultimately reveals how Hitler's used diplomacy to turn his grudges into one-sided treaties, and how he channeled his boundless energy to restore Germany's rightful place as he saw it to a superpower status among its contemporaries.

Against the backdrop of the mountains Hitler utilized rhetorical mechanics in his conversations to get what he wanted: he invoked high pitched tones when making threats, spoke soothingly in a low voice to demonstrate self pity, and conveyed in visually stunning terms the consequence of Europe on fire if he should be denied his destiny of obtaining more living space for Germany. At a barely 5'10" and 150 lb Hitler browbeat his diplomatic guests of larger physical stature into submission.

## LIFE ON THE MOUNTAIN

Propaganda Minister Joseph Goebbels recorded in his diary, found by a Russian officer and hidden in the Soviet archives until 1992, that "the Fuhrer deserves a house that dignified his position as the master of Europe." There was concern though how to pay for such bravado.

In the first few years of his 20 year prison term at Spandau prison Albert Speer struck up a conversation in the prison's garden with Hitler Youth Leader, Baldur von Schirach regard-

ing Hitler's finances. They both reminisced "where the large sums of the money came from to build the Berghof and Eagle's Nest?" Schirach was privy to the fact that official Photographer of the Third Reich, Heinrich Hoffman, informed Hitler to the fact that he could collect royalties of his own image on all the postage stamps issued in Germany. In addition to this a fund was created by Martin Bormann, "The Adolf Hitler Endowment Fund" in which German armament companies were encouraged to donate into to support the Fuhrer's lifestyle in exchange for large armament contracts.[1]

Not only was the Fuhrer's lifestyle supported from the fund but loans were made to Hitler's future neighbors to allow them to finance the building of their chalets near his on the

Obersalzberg. The "Nazi Kingdom" of wealthy subjects included, Hermann Goring, Joseph Goebbels, Rudolf Hess, Albert Speer and Bormann. Each home was decorated to outdo the other. Fine appointments of handmade furniture, custom made tapestries and rugs, Rosenthal and Meissen china and monogram silver service pieces were ubiquitous. The Nazi Kingdom, known to the general populous as the Fuhrer Zone became a reception area for visiting dignitaries, and heads-of-state, a place meant to impress.

On the Obersalzberg Hitler had at his disposal a dedicated house staff and several chauffeurs who maintained his fleet of Mercedes Benzes, including a 12 cylinder 770-K; a luxurious hard top opera car and a triple axel bullet proof touring sedan he used for the first time in 1938 to make his triumphant entry into Vienna, Austria.

Not far from the Berghof Hitler owned a silo shaped tea house, Der Mooslahnkopf to which he made daily excursions. Typically he was accompanied by Amb. Walther Hewel, Foreign Minister Jochiam von Ribbentrop, his photographer Heinrich Hoffman and Eva Braun. Bormann tagged along to ensure no one monopolized the Fuhrer's time. His photographer Hoffman noticed when Hitler arrived he ordered the windows opened. The room cooled from the mountain air. "Hitler loved to make a fire, he would stoke it, throw in logs and sometimes sit in silence and stare into the flames" he wrote in his cynical memoir, "Hitler was my friend."

When Hitler was away his inner circle visited the Kehlstein house at every opportunity. Bormann in particular would go up on Sundays with his family for dinner.

Construction on the Obersalzberg continued throughout the war. At one point Speer and Finance Minister Hjalmar Schacht complained to Hitler that an exorbitant amount of money was being tied up that could be redirected towards the war effort. Hitler did not tolerate any criticism of his faithful deputy and bluntly snarled "I wish I had seven Bormanns." [2]

In the first week of May 1945, when Hitler and Bormann were long dead the occupying allies on the Obersalzberg encountered work crews repairing bomb damage to the Nazi's homes. From the bunker Bormann simply did not tell his laborers to stop working.

## MEETING THE FUHRER
## IN THE EAGLE'S NEST

The first invited dignitary to the Eagle's Nest was French Ambassador Francois Poncet.

When he finally met Hitler inside the Eagle's Nest he thought Hitler looked tired but appeared youthful and animated.

This was typical of what diplomats thought when they met Hitler. Robert Paines' prolific book "The Life and Death of Hitler" writes "most diplomats who met Hitler for the first time thought he looked younger than his fifty years. Had Hitler died in 1939 he would have been eulogized as a political firebrand who restored—albeit illegally—Germany to its former glory and brought it out from the dark shadow cast upon it by the armistice's vestige of the Versailles Treaty."

His followers and critics alike credited him with lifting the German economy out of its post World War I doldrums due mostly to his insistence on re-militarizing Germany in defiance of the Treaty of Versailles.

In the art of diplomacy Hitler had no formal training yet he could converse as if a skilled diplomat. He welcomed and greeted guests with immense confidence and seemed to command any discipline put forth.

Visitors to the Eagle's Nest, many educated at the best universities in Europe were impressed with Hitler's intelligence, if not a little spooked by it. He led conversation by delving into familiar subjects and would converse on famous opera houses or political palaces located in the home town of the visiting guest, he retained world history and was familiar with various styles of art and architecture which allowed him to monopolize conversations recalled Speer. Though Hitler's inquisitiveness can't be ignored either he would often inquire to his visiting guest of the latest fashion trends, movie star gossip or art gallery openings happening in their home capital.

On the evening of September 16. 1938, the inaugural of the Eagle's Nest took place. Bormann threw a party on the peak which was attended by Hitler, Eva Braun, Speers', Nicolaus von Below, Goebbels' and other inner circle regulars.

Hitler commented to von Below: "I will bring up diplomats and heads-of-state I wish to impress."[3] So was the start of Hitler's brief but fateful diplomatic blitzkrieg in the Eagle's Nest.

## II.  SECRET MEETINGS IN THE EAGLE'S NEST

# FIRST CONFERENCE
## FRANCE
## AMB. ANDRÉ FRANCOIS PONCET

## OCTOBER 18, 1938

André François-Poncet was the nearest any non German came to being regarded as a friend of Hitler's. A French politician and diplomat whose post as French ambassador to Germany gave him access to bear witness to the rise of Hitler's Germany. Poncet's father groomed the younger Poncet in German studies at the Paris Institute of Political Studies. He spoke German fluently.

At a pivotal time in the early 1930's when the Nazi Party began to win seats in the German Parliament Poncet was named under secretary of state and ambassador to Germany during his tour as a delegate to the League of Nations in August 1931. In Germany he took notice of the upstart Nazi leader, Adolf Hitler and sent warnings back to France to be aware of this new German rabble rouser who spoke of creating a Third Reich if elected President. Hitler did not win the Presidency in 1933 but was appointed the Vice Presidency, or Chancellor by and under President Paul von Hindenburg. Stationed in Berlin Poncet tried to move in a social circle that would get him close to Hitler, to meet him and ultimately work with him on French-German relations.

The political scene changed drastically when Hindenburg died. Hitler forced the "Enabling Act" through Parliament which essentially did away with Parliament and abolished the office of German president at the same time. He even gave himself a new title: "Der Fuhrer."

Now in charge Hitler took a liking to the French ambassador. Perhaps it was their common experiences of World War I in which Poncet served as an infantry lieutenant between 1917 and 1919.

Poncet found himself invited to the Hitler's Munich's Brown House for coffee. He was also a frequent guest at Reich Chancellery social functions, sat at Hitler's dinner table at the Berghof and was seen in the "Fuhrer Box" at the 1936 Berlin Summer Olympics, which shows the clout he had with Hitler.

In the post Munich Agreement era Hitler decided to try to build alliances with France, Italy, and possibly Poland to begin the dismantling of the English empire. He began by inviting Poncet to the top of the mountain for a meeting on October 18, 1938.

Poncet boarded Hitler's private plane and was flown from Berlin to Salzburg where the Fuhrer's chauffeured Mercedes was waiting. Cruising in the open air sedan Poncet surveyed the Bavarian countryside and recalled a sudden jolt of anxiety after driving past the Fuhrer's house, the Berghof, and continued up a mountain road, unknown and unfamiliar to him.

To his attaché he said "from afar the extraordinary place looked like a hermitage. The Eagle's Nest gave me the impression of being suspended in space; the whole view bathed in autumn dusk, loomed grand, savage, hallucinate. Was this the Castle of Monsalvat, peopled by the knights of the Holy Grail?"[4]

At three o'clock Poncet arrived at the parking place. He walked through the tunnel to the antechamber where an elevator was located deep in the heart of the mountain. The ride took 45 second to the top where the elevator doors opened and Poncet entered the Fuhrer's inner sanctum if there ever was one.

Inside the Eagle's Nest vestibule the "Fuhrer stood there with outstretched arms, he greeted me amiably and with courtesy and seemed very relaxed."[5]

They exchanged cordial pleasantries and expressed enthusiasm about their meeting. Hitler's pleasant demeanor though could not hide the burdening thoughts of war clouding his mind, the "Fuhrer's somber face was pale and fatigued" was Poncet's impression of his host. Initially Poncet questioned why he was here standing on top of a mountain but very soon realized he was to be Hitler's sounding board for his next diplomatic conquest.

Poncet reflected later: "It was an unusual farewell meeting, being reassigned to Rome, he summoned me neither to his Chancellery nor to his Berghof chalet at Berchtesgaden but to his mountain retreat, the Eagle's Nest, his inner circle only and no foreigner had ever visited. In his mind this was a rare favor than I appreciated at the time, the occasion being the last political conversation I was to have with him."[6] In the Great Hall Poncet noticed Roman columns and "huge logs" burning in the fireplace. Under a timber lined ceiling they talked about art and the current trends in Paris. Hitler directed him to a window: "to look out in any direction over the endless panorama of mountains, it was like looking down from an airplane. In the hollow of the amphitheater lay Salzburg and its neighboring villages, dominated as far as the eye traveled by a horizon of chains and peaks with meadows and woods clinging to the slopes."[7]

After inconsequential banter Hitler broached the reason for Poncet's special invitation to the Eagle's Nest. Together they descended into a small room adjacent to the Great Hall, known as the legendary "Eva Braun Tea Room." Here, across a small dining table, arguably, the first true Axis-Allied summit meeting began. True in the sense that both sides pulled

equal diplomatic leverage for Hitler put himself in the unusual position of having to lobby Poncet for French support of
his Nazi foreign policy: "At his order tea was served to which
von Ribbentrop accompanied us while other Nazi familiars
remained aloof in the main room. The servant retired and the
doors closed upon them we began a three party conversation
into which von Ribbentrop entered rarely but always repeated
the Fuhrer's remarks which seemed filled with experience
and wisdom." [8]

Just two weeks after the Czech Sudeten Land had been handed
to him without a shot being fired, Hitler declared the Munich
Agreement a "disappointment." He told Poncet that his gains
from "the Munich Agreement could not dispel the specter of
a future war," because the will of the Nazis is on the march
to colonize more German speaking areas outside of Germany.
Flagrant resistance by the West to his quest for more German
speaking territories would hinder the ability to "mark the beginning of an era of improved relations between the nations."
For two hours Hitler calmly and pointedly cited historical evidence and anecdotes as to why Germany had the right to more
Lebensraum, or living space in the heart of Europe.

Reading from prepared notes Hitler proposed three principles
that, if, they could agree to, would ensure stability between
their governments: First, a mutual foreign policy of recipro-
cal consultation whenever the relations of the countries were
affected; second, the two countries would condemn their historical enemy, the British and its treaties; and third, declare
Britain in violation of international law due to its idea that
it possessed rights to foreign colonies. Over an outstretched
map, Hitler casually swept his hand across borders to "upset
nations and continents like some demigod in his madness."

After listening to the Fuhrer's self-serving monologue Poncet queried a few concerns, which "Hitler answered candidly, sincerely and directly."

Taking a break from the table talk Hitler invited Poncet out to the Kehlstein colonnade for a portrait. From the terrace the Frenchman confessed reluctant admiration for Martin Bormann and Dr. Todt's work, the two who oversaw the massive engineering and construction effort to make the Eagle's Nest.

When the shadow of the mountains began to overtake the Eagle's Nest, Poncet announced his leave. Escorted to the elevator Hitler "expressed his wish to see me again, and several times grasped my hands and shook them warmly. Walking through the underground tunnel I found the car awaiting me at the door." Back on friendly soil Poncet met with the French cabinet to report on his meeting with Europe's most famous politician of the day. He recommended to his superiors that "the Fuhrer can be trusted only with reservation, the main point is how far to go." Furthermore, he expressed empathy for previous heads-of-state who had their textbook diplomatic tactics demolished by the Fuhrer's seemingly rational rhetorical justifications; nevertheless, this is why Poncet admitted that anyone "would have been justified in believing that here was a well-balanced man."[9]

Poncet was wise to Hitler, mainly due to their long-standing professional and cordial association over many years. Looking back he recognized Hitler's political objectives as "contradictory and uncertain, the same man who was good natured in appearance and expressed reasonable opinions on European politics was capable of the wildest frenzies and the most delirious ambitions."[10] The two parted ways in such a manner that neither was pleased with the other.

At his new diplomatic post in Rome, Poncet learned from the ambassadors' circle that Hitler faulted him for failing to show gratitude of the "inspired invitation" to the Eagle's Nest. Poncet responded dryly that "the Eagle's Nest was a billionaire's folly." In his memoirs, Poncet's summation of the Eagle's Nest did not fare much better: "Was it the work of a normal mind or of one tormented by megalomania and haunted by visions of domination and solitude? Or had it been built by a man who was simply prey to his fears."

# THE GOEBBELS' SHOT GUN RECONCILIATION

## OCTOBER 23, 1938

After Poncet's visit Hitler put aside foreign policy to resolve a brewing domestic crisis. He was forced to take notice of the public disintegration of the Goebbels' family and its impact on the integrity of the Party. Choosing a private venue to resolve the crisis Hitler decided to broker a cease-fire between Dr. and Mrs. Goebbels' at the Eagle's Nest.

On October 19, 1939, Magda Goebbels approached Hitler literally on the steps of the Berghof to appeal for his help. She was invited to the Eagle's Nest for tea where Hitler listened to her side of the story.

Later, when Himmler and Nazi Theology Minister Rosenberg approached Hitler on the same subject, that Dr. Goebbels was making a mockery of the Party in the world press, Hitler "had had enough." Not surprisingly, Hitler sided with Mrs. Goebbels because he felt obligated to those, like her, who stuck by the Party during its earliest days of struggle. More importantly, Magda Goebbels was the honorary first lady of the Reich since Hitler did not have a wife, and was determined that his mistress Eva Braun remain unknown to the public.

From the Eagle's Nest Great Hall Hitler called Dr. Goebbels who was attending the opening ceremony of the Hamburg Opera House. Without regard for protocol Goebbels was called away from the event and forced to take the Fuhrer's call. "Your presence is required at the Berghof, tomorrow" recalled Goebbels in his diary.

Hitler instructed Goebbels to stay away from his mistress, Lidora Bavorra, who was under Gestapo surveillance and would be deported. Before retiring for the evening, Goebbels jotted in his diary: "so the situation is finally heating up." Sitting in Hitler's Berghof office, Goebbels pleaded to be "reassigned to Japan with his mistress." Hitler declined and ordered him to return in two days time to take part in reconciliation with his wife and their children at the Eagle's Nest.

The Goebbels showed up at the Berghof on the evening of October 23. "Hitler, Eva Braun, Speers' and Hewel, together, took the gold plated elevator up to the lofty Eagle's Nest to celebrate the shotgun reconciliation."[11] On the top of the mountain, Eva Braun and Margret Speer did their best to keep the situation light hearted. Over coffee and strudel Hitler declared his acceptance of the Goebbels' renewed wedding vows and looked forward to their public reconciliation as well.

Taking Goebbels aside, Hitler sat him down on the big fireplace hearth where the Fuhrer tried to gloss over his anxiety about the reconciliation, but the photograph of the two sitting there betrays Goebbels' uneasiness, and uncertainty. Minutes later Hewel took the famous photograph of the Goebbels' with *Uncle Fuhrer* on the Kehlstein terrace which was distributed to the international press and made into a postcard to show "all was well with the Goebbels' household."

Hitler was pleased, Bavorra was deported, and Magda was still "first lady of the Reich."

And Dr. Goebbels?

Although seemingly innocuous the "forced Goebbels reunion" had tragic consequences for Germany's Jewish community. Because Hitler had cost Goebbels "to lose his love" the propaganda minister became stuck with a wife he no longer wanted. Weeks later Goebbels vented his anger by directing his propaganda agents to smash the windows of Jewish businesses and places of worship throughout Berlin which became known as the infamous Krystal Nacho (Crystal Night). In the end the Party did take responsibility for committing the damage, but it was excused as state sanction retaliation for the murder of a Embassy Secretary in Paris, Ernst von Rath, by a man of Jewish heritage.

Albert Speer reflected in prison on what he saw in 1938, which had given him concern at that time that the open public attack on the Jews was "crossing the Rubicon" into the eventual execution of the Holocaust. Reichsmarschall Hermann Goring, who had a voice of integrity in European politics, saw this savage attack as a political setback for Germany's diplomatic initiatives, although his dismay was for political reasons rather than humanitarian one.

## New Year's Eve, 1938

The inner circle retreated to the Berghof in late December to be with their Fuhrer for the Yuletide season.

After dinner on New Year's Eve, 1938, Bormann, Eva Braun and her sisters ventured up to the Eagle's Nest to ring in January first at 6,000 ft. Arriving at the tunnel they were challenged by a drift of snow covering the tunnel doors. Manning shovels they dug but wound up giving up and returned to the Berghof. Nineteen thirty nine was off to a bad start.

## SECOND CONFERENCE
## LEAGUE OF NATIONS AMBASSADOR
## TO DANZIG,
## CARL J. BURCKHARDT
## AUGUST 10, 1939

After the snow was cleared Hitler went up to the Eagle's Nest on January 4, 1939, to a hold a conference with a visiting Polish delegation, a crucial meeting to look at diplomatic scenarios to avoid war. Foreign Minister, Col. Josef Beck faced Hitler's wrath to hand over the Polish Danzig corridor. Beck diplomatically refused and forced Hitler to ponder his dilemma; Germany would have to march to get the Danzig, but on what pretext could Hitler invade Poland?

Fate turned the Fuhrer's way when a solution presented itself later that summer on August 9, 1939, when word from the Danzig Gaul, Albert Forester reached him that German port workers were being prevented from carrying out their duties due to restriction from Warsaw, the Polish capitol.

There was also a threat circulating that the Danzig authorities were going to close the German operated port leaving German nationals without a source of income.

"From his mountain top hideaway the Fuhrer leaped on it, he got personally involved." He instructed Goebbels to play up the incident as an international violation against the German people. Goebbels' newspapers splashed contrived headlines of Warsaw inspired atrocities against German women and children and that Germans as foreign nationals were denied the chance to earn a fair living. Hitler believed that stories of Danzig officials brutalizing German nationals would justify the right to use might, as such the British and French would unlikely step in to fight on behalf of Danzig.

Hitler first tried to use strong arm diplomacy by inviting the League of Nations Ambassador to Danzig, Carl Burckhardt, to the Eagle's Nest to show he was trying to resolve the matter in good faith.

On August 10, Hitler instructed his Nazi official in Danzig, Forester to interrupt Burckhardt at a dinner he was attending in honor of the Polish General, Tadeusz Perkowski, that "the Fuhrer wanted to meet him on the Obersalzberg at 4 p.m. the next day."

Hitler's private plane was flown in that night to Warsaw and was ready for Burckhardt to board in the morning.

On the way he had to endure an hour of Forester's animated in-flight stories about the early Party days when the Fuhrer led the beer hall fights against the Communists. After landing, the diplomat was given a quick breakfast and informed they were "going to the Eagle's Nest, the recently built house in the dizzying heights of the mountain peaks."

The purpose of this interview was not so much to negotiate a peaceful resolution to the Danzig crisis as much as it was for Hitler to appear he was using the international organization to right a wrong. In a way Burckhardt's invitation was Hitler's machination to show off his monumental engineering achievement, it exemplified Nazi will power to conquer a mountain, and if need be conquer any resistance to him and his mission.

But prior to Burckhardt's arrival Hitler was preoccupied with another issue. Early in the morning Speer rode with Hitler in the Fuhrer's Mercedes and recalled how this thrilling drive up to the Eagle's Nest became even more extraordinary: "About the beginning of August we, an untroubled group drove with Hitler up to the Eagle's Nest. The long motorcade wound along the road Bormann had blasted into the rock. Through a high bronze portal we entered the marble hall damp from the moisture. At the heart of the mountain we stepped into an elevator lift of polished brass. As we rode up, as if talking to him Hitler said something important will happen soon. Even if I have to send Goring . . . but if need be I'll go myself to meet Stalin...staking everything on this card."[12]

His reference to "perhaps something enormous important will happen" refers to diplomatic feelers in Moscow and their mission to get Stalin's signature on a "German-Russian nonaggression pact," an agreement that would split the Polish frontier between the two, making Stalin an ally not an adversary.

In the afternoon Burckhardt arrived. On top of the mountain the foreign policy meeting between the Nazi Party and the League of Nations began.

Stepping into the Great Hall the first person Burckhardt saw was Albert Speer, sedate and slumped in a chair. Without greeting his guest, Hitler paced the expanse of the Great Hall, "working himself into frenzy," spewing threats of retaliation against an unnamed foe. The perception of the mighty and masterful Fuhrer was quickly deflated when one of the serving staff dropped a heavy armchair on his foot and had him hopping in pain.[13]

The sudden impact seemed to jolt him back to reality; he called for modest demands and stressed that the Poles' need for Western support (Britain or France) against him was not necessary. Then Burckhardt stepped into Hitler's line of fire: "If the slightest thing happens (violence committed against German nationals) without warning I would pounce on the Poles like lighting, and with all the power of a mechanized force which they never dreamed of." Jolted but calm Burckhardt responded: "I understand Monsignor Chancellor I quite realize this means a general war," as if to call his bluff. Hitler sat down at his coffee table, he looked visibly pained.[14]

He continued: "Very well. If I am forced into this conflict I will not conduct it like Wilhelm II, with scruple of conscience before waging total war, I will fight relentlessly to the bitter end." Hitler went on to warn: "Resistance from Poland would be useless; a technical defense force of cavalry was no match for a fortification of 74 divisions that could hold any western line that would defend Poland. My generals' hesitant years before are now ready to go against the Poles. I do not bluff."[15]

Standing up from his chair he told Burckhardt to follow him out to the covered colonnade, a tactic he used last October to ease stressed moments during his talks with French Amb. Poncet. On the terrace they peered across the endless horizon, the jagged Alps stabbed the blue-sky.

Hitler, as if thinking out loud, said "I have endured enough turmoil," and desired "peace and quiet." "Peace" would be welcomed throughout Europe retorted Burckhardt, but "this lay in your hands more than any other person." "Not so" Hitler replied in a low voice. Nevertheless, if he found out that England and France were going to support Poland in its defiance then he would "prefer war this year as oppose to next." Burckhardt had heard enough; he wished the Fuhrer well and abruptly took the gold and brass elevator down to his waiting car.

In the days after the meeting, with no alliances beside token agreements with Italy and Japan Hitler was visibly anxious, was prone to emotional outbursts and showed indecisive intentions. Speer observed how Hitler's self-assurance and confidence escaped him during the tense times prior to invading Poland.

Two days later Burckhardt invited Roger Matkin from the British Foreign Office, and Pierre Arnal of the Quaid'Orsay, to meet at of all places, his mother's home, to ensure secrecy. He relayed to his diplomatic colleagues that he found the "Fuhrer extremely upset at press suggestions that he had lost his nerve and was forced to give way about the Polish customs officers treatment of German nationals.

"Hitler may negotiate on the Danzig issue. But it will be another matter if the press revile him and cover him in ridicule" shared Burckhardt and he was concerned for Hitler's mental and physical well-being: "he appeared much older than the last time they met two years earlier. Hitler was nervous, anxious, and apparently undecided." Burckhardt felt confident that Hitler may not go to war "if the Poles pick up and leave Danzig in peace, and provide Germany with much needed grain and timber."[16] Though Burckhardt's intentions were good von Ribbentrop confirmed at the Nuremberg trial that "Hitler's diplomatic efforts in 1939 were window dressing, we wanted war."

When Hitler was meeting with Burckhardt that day in the Eagle's Nest, von Ribbentrop was softening up Il Duce and his son-in-law, Count Galeazzo Ciano, at his newly acquired residence at Fuschl Lake a few miles from the Eagle's Nest.

Since the Polish government was not going to roll over and simply be annexed like Austria was Hitler was anxious to meet with Mussolini the next day to ask him to ally with Germany in the invasion of Poland. Hitler desperately wanted to move east, towards Russia.

Now Hitler had a plan.

# THIRD CONFERENCE
## ITALY
## COUNT GALEAZZO CIANO
## AUGUST 11, 1939

On a sunny but cold August morning von Ribbentrop delivered Count Ciano to the foot of the Berghof's ceremonial stairs where an SS honor guard provided a State welcome. Typically a honor guard is reserved for visiting heads of state, however, Hitler's confidant and friend Il Duce was a no show.

Visibly disappointed Hitler greeted Count Ciano, dressed resplendently in his white military uniform, his hat at a jaunty angle; he saluted the Fuhrer and they proceeded up the Berghof stair way. Hitler escorted Ciano to the Berghof's reception hall; its famous window was rolled down into the wall for a stunning panoramic view of the Alps. Natural light washed across large maps of Europe spread out on the table.

Trying not to reveal his displeasure at having to deal with Ciano instead of Mussolini, Hitler got to the heart of the matter. He confidently predicted that in a matter of days his crack German Wehrmact and Luftwaffe would smash the Pole's outdated army, though he would value and appreciate back up of Italy's military.

"Surprisingly Ciano stood up to Hitler" and refused to commit. "Italy wasn't prepared for a general war," its economy was too soft, its currency weak. They exchanged rhetorical barbs and Hitler went for a diversion, lunch.

Trying to keep the discussion informal Ciano began poking fun at the floral arrangements, probably made by Eva Braun. After lunch they returned to the map table. It was no use; the Count was not buying Hitler's argument for a quick and painless kill. In response Ciano put the truth forward, Italy would last a month in a state of war, even if it was a small generalized war, furthermore, his father-in-law, Mussolini wanted the Polish question solved by conference—not conflict and believed Hitler's invasion of Poland would propel Europe into a new World War.

Predictably, the start of their meeting went nowhere. Hitler and Ciano's relationship was always contentious: Hitler thought Ciano drank too much, and Ciano saw Hitler for what he was, a corporal.

Adding to the uneasiness is that Ciano did not trust Hitler and Ribbentrop by nature, and had trouble accepting their Nazi hospitality. Hitler sensed it, and "with all affability suggested they postpone further talks until morning and drive up to his retreat on the Kehlstein while there was still good light."[17]

Notably, this was a rare time when Hitler wore his military tunic to the summit, and for the first time, brought a representative from the military branch with him to back up his rhetoric. Reichsmarschall Goring sent his Adjutant, Col. Von Below (Goring and Bormann could not be in the same room for any length of time) who stayed at the Fuhrer's hip to reinforce statistical strength and the Luftwaffe's superior numbers whenever Ciano cited the British RAF as a fair opponent.

Inside the Great Hall Hitler lured his guest toward one of the windows. Ciano acted unimpressed. When Hitler pressed him about the "expansive views" Ciano just shivered as if he was freezing. Offered tea to warm up Ciano only made a sour face, though he drank cup after cup. That night Ciano retired to his suite at Bormann's Gästehaus Hoher Göll, a large chalet next to the Berghof.

Sitting at a writing desk in his room he took in the incredible view of the Untersberg Mountain while phoning his father-in-law to recount the evening's meeting: "I am certain that even if the Germans were given more than they ask for they would attack just the same because they are possessed by the demons of destruction."[18]

In the morning he took the roughed out path connecting the guest house to the Berghof. At the Fuhrer's breakfast table he was asked again to have Italy commit to the invasion of Poland. This time Ciano "folded like a jackknife." He had a change of heart, because "you see things more clearly than we do."

Exuberant, Hitler called his foreign office to find out the status of the nonaggression pact put forth to Stalin. Hitler's concern was that Stalin might sign a trade agreement with a British delegation that was on its way to Moscow. Ribbentrop was given his marching order by Hitler: "reach an understanding with Stalin at once."

Eight days after Ciano left the Eagle's Nest Stalin agreed not to interfere with Hitler's invasion of Poland. Speer witnessed the moment. While at dinner at the Berghof a military aide handed the Fuhrer a message. Hitler slammed his fists on the table and yelled, "I have them." The rest of the meal went on in silence. After dinner the inner circle gathered around Hitler at the big fireplace. "Here, read this telegram, it's from Stalin" Hitler gestured. Champagne was served.[19]

On the afternoon of August 22, 1939, Hitler gathered his senior commanders in the Berghof's Great Hall to share his foreign policy response to the "unbearable situation with Poland." It was at this time that he revealed the invasion date of Poland.

40

# FOURTH CONFERENCE
## ITALY
## PRINCESS MARIA JOSE,

## HITLER'S LAST VISIT

## OCTOBER 17, 1940

Hitler visited the Eagle's Nest on October 17, 1940, for a special meeting with Italian Princess, Maria Jose.

With Europe at Hitler's feet the Nazis were pleased to have an authentic princess of royalty requesting the Furher's favor of a meeting. Hitler offered the princess lunch at his diplomat's house and brought along his photographer to document the event.

Princess Jose was married to Prince Umberto of Italy's Royal family; she requested a meeting with Hitler on behalf of her brother, Belgium's King Leopold, to lobby the Fuhrer to release Belgium prisoners-of-war recently detained by the German army after the invasion and occupation of Belgium.

Her attempt was futile, and even naive, but admirable. Hitler essentially appeared to listen to his guest but really did nothing to fulfill her request. It was a merely a propaganda coup for him to have his picture taken with a princess at his round table. Interestingly he dignified his guest by not wearing his military tunic and not wearing his swastika arm band. In his suit he appeared as head-of-state rather than dictator, and did comment later that the princess had more guts than many of the male diplomats who called on him.

Other than Hitler's offhand remark to von Below that he looked forward to using the Eagle's Nest for upcoming meetings, the visit by Princess Maria Jose confirms that Hitler thought well of the Eagle's Nest and proudly shared the Nazi fairy tale castle with royalty.

# III. WORLD WAR II:  THE FUHRER DEFUNCT

# THE EAGLE'S NEST WEDDING RECEPTION
## SS OBERGRUPPENFUHRER
## HERMANN FEGELEIN
## AND GRETL BRAUN

## JUNE 3, 1944

By June 1944 the Russian Front was rapidly moving towards Hitler's Wolf's Lair, his front line bunker and command post. The mosquito infested Fuhrer hideout would need to be reinforced with more concrete by Speer's construction crews. Hitler got on his train and went to the Berghof for the last time.

As the war got closer Foreign Minister von Ribbentrop tried to get Hitler to negotiate with the British, to sue for a temporary peace long enough to hurl the western front against the eastern onslaught of the Red Army. Ribbentrop confessed to his Nuremberg jailers that Fuhrer had aged, he had a pronounced stoop and was seemingly lethargic towards everything and everyone. Goebbels too noted in his journal that his Fuhrer had become war weary: his body and mind seem to be revolting; in particular he blamed Dr. Theodor Morrell's medical voodoo.

Even though Morrell was much maligned the Fuhrer swore by his doctor's daily cocktail injections of amphetamines, sedatives and eye drops laced with cocaine. All in all, Hitler still believed in his "star," and his inner circle reluctantly shared in his enthusiasm.

In early June reports filtered in from Himmler's spies in England of a buildup of Anglo-American forces along the English Channel. Becoming pre-occupied with the likelihood of an invasion Eva Braun tried to detour his attention to the upcoming wedding of her sister. She asked his permission to allow

Gretl and soon to be husband, SS Obergruppenfuhrer Hermann Fegelein to have their reception in the Eagle's Nest.

He acquiesced, however, declined to attend because he wanted to listen to the BBC radio broadcast for the "secret signals" that would tip off the French underground that the invasion was commencing. To that end the bride and groom had to settle for a photograph with the Fuhrer in the Berghof's Great Hall.

On the evening of June 3, 1944, Bormann drove the lead Mercedes with the bride and groom and a procession of twenty cars up the winding road to the Eagle's Nest. Some fifty guests attended. Music was provided by Himmler's own SS band, and the party went on for two days, including the nights of June 4 and 5.

On leaving the Eagle's Nest in the early morning hours of June 6, the party goers learned of the Normandy invasion.

During the early morning of June 6, the general staff asked that the Fuhrer be awaken but none of his adjutants dare. No one wanted to be accused of judging the situation wrongly. Hitler emerged from his room on his own at noon.

Throughout June 6, Hitler chose to ignore reports of a bad situation getting worse. In the afternoon he asked Speer to walk with him to his small teahouse, Mooslahnkopf, as they had done so often in the early days of glory. Now they "walked in silence each dwelling on his own thoughts" remembered Speer. On arrival they took their seats around the table, in the glow of the fire Hitler said he "welcomed the fight."

Hitler took a call from Goring and dismissed any thought that there was allied superiority; after all Rommel's brilliant military genius would repeal the invaders back into the sea. Hitler's generals saw it another way: the inevitable Russian offensive would begin shortly and with the Allied invasion there would be no chance for a turn of events.

Goring, in particular warned Hitler about taking on a two front war.

Sides began to form: one for Hitler, and the other against. Enter Obergruppenfuhrer Hermann Fegelein, who stood by his Fuhrer through the D-Day invasion and through the attempted assassination the following month on July 20, further raising his esteem in the eyes of his Fuhrer and Hitler's entourage.

Fegelein, 38, a swashbuckling, ambitious character had the coveted power position as Himmler's liaison man to Hitler, a position he earned after narrowly escaping death at Stalingrad. However, at the Berghof he did more socializing than work and made use of his "war hero" status to marry Eva Braun's sister.

Marrying into the Braun family had consequences, if the war was loss. Case in point when in a year's time he was expected to uphold family loyalty and commit suicide in the Fuhrer Bunker with his infamous in-laws to avoid capture by the Russians.

On April 27, 1945, Fegelein escaped the bunker hoping to save his skin. Unfortunately, his boss Himmler was identified the next day on the BBC as initiating capitulation talks with the allies in direct violation of Hitler's order: no surrender.

The next day Hitler called for Fegelein to shed some light on his boss' behavior but couldn't be found. Hitler shouted at his own adjutant, Gunsche, "get me Fegelein. Fegelein. Fegelein." An SS squad found him at his Berlin apartment and brought him back to the bunker along with a cache of Eva's jewelry, which he took as a convertible currency since the Reich Mark was worthless. Hitler stripped his "brother-in-law" of his rank and ordered his summarily execution by firing squad in the Reich's Chancellery garden. Speer recalled that machineguns were used.

# BOMBING THE BERGHOF, APRIL 1945

During the last days of the war Hitler had Bormann order the Obersalzberg SS guards to set fire to the Berghof while Julius Schaub made his way to the mountain to destroy the Fuhrer's papers and personal effects. Before Schaub arrived the guards allowed locals to loot the interior and to empty the storeroom of food, liquor and delicacies enough to last 10 years.

A few days later on May 4, the Seventh Infantry Regiment out of the Third Infantry Division reached the Obersalzberg ahead of the 101st Airborne Division and ahead of the Second French Armored Division. Under SS sniper fire the adventurous soldiers of the Seventh Division rushed the Berghof's flagpole to tear down the swastika flag.

After securing the Berghof the roving band of brothers walked around the Nazi neighborhood to discover plentiful war booty, fit for the taking.

Up a hill they entered Reichsmarschall Goring's house. Underneath it was a marble walled bunker, adorned with gold eagles clutching swastikas; this is where Goring stored his premium wine cache of 10,000 bottles that he collected from all over Europe. Hitler's wine vault was more predictable and unassuming, just the standard Moet Chandon, according to Speer.

The next day the Seventh Infantry was ordered to move onto Salzburg, Austria, and relinquished the Berghof and the untouched Eagle's Nest to the 101st Airborne Div. On May 6th the 101st AB began heading up the Kehlstein Road to Hitler's fabled castle on the mountain.

Leading the way was commanding officer, Colonel Sink. Arriving at the large parking place they found the tunnel entrance covered by snowdrifts. Undeterred they took the footpath up to the Eagle's Nest front door. Because of the remote location no one had yet looted the pavilion.

The Eagle's Nest was found in such a way that one could imagine Hitler arriving at any moment.

Everything was in its place: photo albums and stationary were in desk drawers, a cache of monogram 'AH' silver service pieces with the national eagle clutching the swastika was hidden behind a wall panel in the dining room, and many settings of Meissen porcelain dinnerware were stored in oak chests. In a storeroom below the Great Hall were carefully packed crates. One crate contained postcard size watercolors depicting tranquil scenes of grass and trees, city streets with stick figures, and landscapes of snow-capped mountains. This cache was the young Hitler's "frames fillers" he proliferated on the streets of Vienna to make a modest living during the 1910-20's.

Also packed away were a dozen of aquarelles depicting the Eagle's Nest interior room and exterior elevations. These were created by Hitler between 1936 and 1940, the last water color depicted the redecorating of the Great Hall. These watercolors of the Eagle's Nest appear as story boards, sequentially numbered and initialed "AH". On the reverse of each watercolor he wrote the title or descriptive phrase to identify the purpose of the room. The watercolors were not only art but were architectural renderings to depict how the building should appear.

One of those storyboards has on the verso in Hitler's handwriting, "die grosse lasse" or "the big den" which diplomats referred to as the Great Hall. This watercolor appears on the cover of this book. Bormann took this and all the watercolors to his interior designer in Munich to execute Hitler's wishes as to how the Eagle's Nest should appear. Later, Bormann packed the watercolors up with the intention to exhibit them in the new "Fuhrer Museum" in Linz, to be built after the war. This collection became the property of one GI in the 506th PIR who took ownership; he now owned a collection of *Hitlers*.

While the watercolors were the most coveted souvenir in the form of war booty, there were other items collected and traded during May 1945, and the dictum "finders keepers," was the rule of the day. A few enlisted got carried away by claiming ownership to Hitler's Mercedes. Only reluctantly did they turn over the keys to the top brass. In most cases though the men who carried the guns in the field got to keep their prizes of monogram silver service pieces, President Harry S Truman smiled broadly on the lawn of the White House when he was presented with Reichsmarschall Goring's diamond and ruby encrusted Luftwaffe baton, Goring handed it over to his captors in its felt lined case upon his surrender.

At the same time the Obersalzberg was overrun with war criminals. The Allied Command put a damper on the collecting party by issuing orders for the capture of "war criminals" on the Obersalzberg. Helping the allies' snare one of the top Nazis was a priest near Berchtesgaden who notified the 502nd PIR of a "notable man sleeping in a merchant's shop in Berchtesgaden." HQ dispatched a lieutenant, a sergeant, and a private--first class, to visit the shop to check out the odd character.

On the second floor they encountered and arrested the Director of the German Work Force, Robert Ley. Ley hanged himself in his jail cell to escape his responsibility and the justice of the Nuremberg trial that his codefendants Goring, Hess and others would have to endure.

# THE ALLIES TAKE THE EAGLE'S NEST

## POST SCRIPT:
## DEVELOPING THE FUHRER FACADE

At the beginning of the Fuhrer's political career diplomats from the democracies made the sojourn to Berlin and Munich to meet this rising German politician. Throughout the 1930's Hitler enjoyed pressing the flesh with those who came from afar to see him. Beside diplomats he would stroll down the Berghof driveway to meet and greet throngs of admirers.

Being photographed was allowed and encouraged. The top henchmen were comfortable in their own skin, the likes of Hitler, Gobbles and Goring were content to allow their voters and the world to see them sitting around. When Hitler and Goring were not sitting in their chalet living rooms signing autographs, they were photographed going places in their cars, leaving on airplanes, or browsing in car dealer show-rooms. The Nazi propaganda office cranked out thousands of postcards of these banal scenes and circulated them through-out the Germany and to the west.

On the other hand the wrong image could hurt the cult of per-sonality, so photographer Heinrich Hoffman was forbidden from distributing images of the Fuhrer wearing glasses, pet-ting small dogs and being near anyone who wasn't "Nazi."

The innocuous perception of the *Fuhrer façade* was the mach-ination of Hoffman and perpetrated through the propaganda of Goebbels who posed their boss in scenes of tranquil famil-iarity in an effort to portray him as a benevolent despot.

Hoffman's controlled distribution reveals images of Ger-many's leadership appearing affable and approachable which paid off when Hitler happen upon villagers and diplomats who rushed forward to shake hands with him. However, photo censorship prevailed. The photographic evidence, the consequence of Hitler's foreign policy and his war are missing from the captured Third Reich official photo collection: that is, missing is any evidence of the death and destruction wrought by his demonic orders. In particular, his SS, when they appear in pictures are shown in snappy, well-pressed uniforms, mostly holding back well-wishers around the Fuhrer. *Their* victims in Dachau and later the death camps are nowhere to be found in the albums.

To Italy's Count Ciano's credit, he, early on peeled away the rhetoric and exposed the evil lurking behind the *Fuhrer façade.* His memoirs' reveal that he shared with his father-in-law, Benito Mussolini, on the night of August 12, 1939, that "even if Hitler got what he wanted he would attack all the same because the Nazis are possessed by the demon of destruction." When the war took a hard, irreversible turn against the Axis Ciano participated in the overthrow of his father-in-law, Mussolini. He was executed for treason.

Further examination of the captured photo albums reveal that during the 1930's Hitler kept one foot in the world of diplomacy and the other in the realm of a potential warlord. During the 1938 diplomatic meetings in the Eagle's Nest Hitler appeared often in a suit and tie, like a civilian head of state, he stressed his eagerness to be Europe's "champion of peace," as if his tailored jacket and trousers was his uniform of official power, suggesting civility, diplomacy and physical self-control.

Less than a year after the Munich Agreement and its result of a wobbly peace agreement, Hitler began to voice militaristic means to meet his objectives; the concept of diplomacy and its subtleties were on their way out, as he infamously quipped: "I saw our enemies at Munich, they're worms."

By late summer of 1939 he discarded his suit and ties and promised the public to wear only a military uniform until the war was over; this symbolized his supreme authoritative status as Fuhrer. In a rare reversal of a personal promise Hitler discarded his uniform during the war to wear a civilian suit for a luncheon meeting he had at the Eagle's Nest with Italy's House of Savoy princess on October, 17, 1940. By the next day the time for talk was over, he never went back to the Eagle's Nest.

# APPENDICES

I.    Official Visits to the Eagle's Nest

II.    Collecting Third Reich Assets

III.    Martin Bormann: God of the Obersalzberg

IV.    Joseph Goebbels: Lie with A Smile

V.    Hermann Goring: 10,000 Wine Bottles

VI.    Coffee. Tea and a War of Words

VII.    Acknowledgement

VIII.    About the Photographs

# OFFICIAL VISITS TO THE EAGLE'S NEST

## *1938*

| | |
|---|---|
| Sept 16: | Hitler makes inaugural visit. |
| Sept 17: | British Journalist Ward Price, Goebbels and Himmler visit. |
| Sept 19: | Hitler visits. |
| Oct 16: | Hitler visits. |
| Oct 17: | Hitler visits. |
| Oct 18: | First Conference: Nazi - French Summit meeting with Amb. François Poncet. |
| Oct 21: | Magda Goebbels meets with Hitler. |
| Oct 23: | Goebbels reconcile their marriage. Attended by Hitler, Braun, Speers.. |
| Oct 24: | C-in-C Walther von Brauchitsch is instructed to "get to grips with his job," or else. |

## *1939*

| | |
|---|---|
| Jan 4: | Meeting with Polish envoy Joseph Beck. |
| July 15: | Labor Minister Dr Ley and Mrs Ley meet with Hitler to discuss war time labor strategies. Goebbels', Eva Braun, others present. |
| Aug 10: | Second Conference: Nazi - League of Nation Summit meeting with Amb. Carl J. Burckhardt. |
| Aug 11: | Third Conference: Nazi - Italy Summit meeting with Count Galeazzo Ciano. |

*1940*

Oct 17:      Fourth Conference. Princess Maria Jose (sister of Belgium King Leopold) requests release of Belgium POW's during a luncheon.

*1944*

June 3:      Wedding Reception: Gretl Braun and SS Obergruppenfuhrer Hermann Fegelein

*1945*

Sept 2:      Gens Eisenhower and Mark Clark visit the Eagle's Nest. Ike removes the "officers only" sign at elevator.

# COLLECTING THIRD REICH'S ASSETS

As is typical for heads-of-state, and Hitler was no different, powerful guys acquire big cars, large estates, art work, fancy silver service pieces and good cigars to fulfill their sense of self importance. These material effects are utilized when entertaining and hosting events of the diplomatic nature. When the allies began to overrun the Reich, GI collectors under the umbrella of the Potsdam Agreement had cart blanch to cart away Nazi possessions.

The homes of Goring, Goebbels, and Hitler's own Munich apartment and his Berghof were overrun and looted by young soldiers who became pretty good at finding prizes. *These collectors* found Goring and Hitler's inventories of wine, personal firearms, uniforms, sets of gold cuff links, engraved watches and in the garages, fleets of Mercedes Benzes. Of interest was the fact that Hitler kept cigars, cigarettes and tobacco in State silver service humidors, monogrammed with "AH," with an embossed eagle and its talons clutching a wreath on the lids. Bormann placed these boxes at the Berghof, Eagle's Nest, Reich Chancellery, the Fuhrerbau (Munich) and his Munich apartment. Most of these humidors have been "collected" and periodically are put on the auction block. The humidors were part of a unique set of the silver service pieces, including, lemon squeezers, lobster picks, martini shakers, tea and coffee service, platters and place settings. A Grecian key surrounding the border of each piece and the "AH" monogram identify them as the "Formal State Pattern."

The humidors and boxes are stamped with "925" for its silver weight and have the maker's mark as well (on the bottom-underside). The box sits on four art deco type legs, lined with Spanish cedar and a piano hinge makes a tight closure.

# MARTIN BORMANN
## GOD OF THE OBERSALZBERG

Martin Bormann did not like any one. No one liked him.

Goring, Goebbels and Speer avoided him. "A man of no culture," recalled Speer. Eva Braun crossed her arms when approached by him. SS Reichsfuhrer Heinrich Himmler formed a rare alliance with Bormann that allowed the latter to oversee the Obersalzberg's SS guards. In return Himmler got direct access to Hitler and did not have to make an appointment as everyone else had to, except Speer.

Bormann controlled total access to Hitler. A password which was actually a phrase was required by Bormann's guards at the Berghof's gate, which was: "An officer's uniform is not a right to see the Fuhrer."

Bormann was drafted into the Field Artillery Regiment 55 near the end of World War I, but saw no action. After the armistice he was unemployed and joined the Nazi Party to begin channeling his ambition into politics.

When Hitler was appointed Chancellor in 1933 Bormann was promoted to deputy to Rudolf Hess, one of Hitler earliest and most loyal lieutenants. Bormann found his niche when Hess's office was given the assignment to land acquisition on the Obersalzberg, to buy up the land surrounding the Fuhrer's house. Hess handed the responsibility to Bormann.

This project was perfect for Bormann. Using the power of his "brown uniform," he put on his hiking boots and walked the roads, stroll the valleys and climbed the mountains including the Kehlstein that overshadowed Hitler's house. With the architect Prof Roderick Fick and the famous Autobahn builder, Prof Todt in tow, they chose the spot where the Eagle's Nest conference room would be built based on a view through an imaginary window. Bormann pounded in the stakes outlining the octagon room. To get to the summit he told his crew that he wanted an elevator shaft bore through the mountain.

Coming down from the mountain Bormann began knocking on farm house doors in the effort to start growing the Fuhrer Zone. At first he would politely offer money for the property. Some took it and moved on. Some were allowed to think about it. Those who refused to sell in turn received a letter on "Deputy Fuhrer M. Bormann" letterhead indicating either "sell or be relocated to Dachau without reimbursement." These letters earned Bormann the dubious distinction of being the feared "god of the Obersalzberg."

Bormann's building spree began in 1936 and continued to the literally the last days of the war.

Even when the German economy showed signs of weakness Hitler allowed Bormann to tie up thousands of workers and approved 30 million RM's "donated from the armament industry" to pay for the construction of the Eagle's Nest. Speer later recounted that "the Obersalzberg was a goldmine into which gold was being put into, not taken out of."

Hitler had very little involvement in planning and building the Eagle's Nest. After the war invoices were found in Bormann's administration offices that show construction cost exceeding $30m Reichsmarks, or $100,000,000 in US dollars. The interior design and appointments (furniture, rugs, tapestries, State pattern silver service) cost another $250,000 USD.

A loyal servant to his Fuhrer Bormann though chose to escape the bunker tomb a day after his boss committed suicide there. In 1972 a construction crew working near the Berlin Lehrter railroad station found a set of bones buried a few feet deep in the soil. The dental records matched Bormann's. It's likely

Bormann and his entourage, just a half mile from the Reich Chancellery had to back track on the railroad while coming face to face with Russian patrol, he was either killed by shrapnel or bit a poison capsule.

## JOSEPH GOEBBELS
## LIE WITH A SMILE

Joseph Goebbels was a onetime communist thug, who antagonized the Nazis at rallies and meetings in the early Weimer Republic days; however, when the Nazi Party's star began to rise on the political scene the opportunist Goebbels cast his lot with his new god, Adolf Hitler and the Nazi Party.

The relationship between Hitler and Goebbels even during the Nazi hey days was not always amicable. At one time in 1938 Goebbels was actually placed under "house arrest" on the Fuhrer's orders. In exchange for his freedom Hitler demanded that he give up his girlfriend and behave like a married man.

Goebbels' genius, albeit evil, was his ability to grasp an idea and give it life through rhetoric. He coined the phrase "Iron Curtain," not Winston Churchill when he wrote in his journal on March 23, 1944, about the Soviets advance across Europe and Germany: "an iron curtain has dropped across Europe."

Goebbels was also a realist. Unlike Himmler who were deluded with vision of leadership in post War II Germany, Goebbels saw the hangman's noose swinging in front of him. He chose to kill himself to avoid the dishonor of signing a Russian instrument of surrender. His last word on departing the Berlin bunker -- and life were: "the die is cast."

## HERMANN GORING
## 10,000 WINE BOTTLES.

He was the first Obersalzberger.

He began visiting the area in 1920 and stayed in a small chalet on the side of the Kehlstein. The Kehlstein was a sporting area enjoyed by Goring where he usually hunted and rock climbed (he was agile and in-shape in his younger years).

Initially his chalet was little more than a shack, however, after securing political power he staked out a hill area on the Obersalzberg and built an immense sprawling mansion, decorated with artwork plundered from Europe. In his front yard he set up an archer's target and had a swimming pool installed.

Goring was useful to Hitler in that he brought integrity to the Party through his connections with industrialists and royalty. He was comfortable with pretentious diplomats and had the diplomats' appreciation for good cigars and expensive wine. He was in effect Hitler's defacto lead diplomat.

As a result Hitler let him indulge his pleasures, such as Bormann loaning Goring funds to build a marble lined cellar under his house to keep his 10,000 bottles of French wine and champagne. The 101st Airborne Division liberated most of the cache in May 1945, destroying each bottle, one by one. Goring was a popular figure on the Obersalzberg and was greeted by the local population when strolling or driving around the Obersalzberg. Because he and Bormann despised each other Goring avoided the Eagle's Nest like the plague. There exist no photographs of him visiting the Eagle's Nest as Goring could never show appreciation of his nemesis' project.

# COFFEE, TEA AND A WAR OF WORDS:
# SEPT 17, 1938.

Hitler had undeniable star appeal to the press. He looked odd, and was prone to outbursts. "He had a funny hairdo" wrote President Herbert Hoover who met Hitler in his Berlin office. Journalists tracked his moves from Berlin to Nuremberg, Munich to Italy and back to the Obersalzberg, in anticipation of a controversial quote.

It was common for journalist to hang outside his Munich and Berlin office. On occasion Adjutant Julius Schaub would announce that "the Third Reich was leaving for Berchtesgaden in a few minutes." Soon, a fleet of Mercedes Benz 770's emerged from the Reich Chancellery garage, and the race to Bavaria was on. The journalist cars could not compete with the Fuhrer's convoy of 12 cylinder Mercedes Benzes as they stormed by. The SS guards hanging out the windows.

At the Obersalzberg, on the early afternoon of September 17, 1938, journalist Ward Price called the Berghof's press office to see what was on the Fuhrer's schedule. Schaub informed Price that the "Fuhrer is having lunch with Dr. Goebbels and will be going up to the Kehlstein." After a pause he added, "the Fuhrer wishes for you to attend."

Hitler wanted to show off his prized birthday present to this foreign journalist in particular and to cast rhetorical barbs at Ward's Prime Minister, Neville Chamberlain, who was at the Berghof two day before. Inside the Great Hall they sat in big goose down chairs facing the fireplace. Tea and coffee were served in Meissen china with red dragon motifs. Hitler was congenial to a point but suddenly talked across Price to Dr. Goebbels as if Price was not there.

Hitler accused the "British as being political colonizers" and viciously described the prime minister as wolf in sheep's clothes who "carried an umbrella to disguise his shrewdness." Ward choked on his crumpets as Hitler snarled that the British had colonies throughout the world just to feed its subjects and for tea to brew; then intimated that Germany likewise would need Czechoslovakia to meet its own needs.

Goebbels was shocked. "The war of nerves has begun," Goebbels wrote in his journal, not quite sure why the Fuhrer wanted to aggravate an already volatile situation. But Hitler calculated that Price would report back to Chamberlain that Germany was leaning towards belligerence and that diplomacy may have run its course. Time was running out an the press was privy to this fact.

## ACKNOWLEDGEMENT

In the "I got to thank you department" I extend my gratitude to those who helped in content matter, photo research and lending ideas to this project.

Honorable mentions include: Mike and Cindy at Do You Graphics; Sgt William Eckert (ret) for use of his photo library; thanks to Mr. Bass at the Robert Culver Library; Henrike Kampfe at Bavarian State Library; Getty Life Images; and, Brig Gen John S.D. Eisenhower for sharing his memories with me.

Thank you to Mr. and Mrs. Donald Mossman without who I would be impossible.

To Mary Pirus for inspiration, and to my Mary Clancy for encouragement, love and support. Thank you Monroe! Thank you to my typist, O'key who put in many long nights with me at the keyboard. Thanks Honey and Eva for being there too.

Thank you Gens Eisenhower, Patton, MacArthur, George C. Marshall and the American soldier who took on Hitler and his gang and beat them.

# ABOUT THE PHOTOGRAPHS

1. Eagle's Nest on the Mountain. 1945. This photo comes from the Library of Congress. The notation in the card catalog indicates this photo was handed to an attendee of the Nuremberg trials while visiting the Obersalzberg.

2. Eagle's Nest from the Sky. Ariel Photo by the U.S. Air Force, 1945.

3. Tunnel to Elevator. 1938. A well circulated pre-war postcard, the parking lot at the tunnel entrance is where guests were left off and walked deep into the tunnel to an elevator. Only Hitler's Mercedes drove into the tunnel. Later his car would back in and drive straight out with the Fuhrer in the front seat.

4. Modern Day Eagle's Nest Vista, 2005.

5. Hitler at the Eagle's Nest Door. 1939. It was rare that Hitler was photographed outside the Eagle's Nest; this is the only known photo of him at the "front door." The clouds behind him obstruct an awesome panoramic view. The armband is surprisingly attire, in most photos he appears in a suit and tie, like a diplomat.

6. Albert Speer, Margrete Speer and Eva Braun. 1940. The round table, to the left, set for dinner was installed in 1940 at Hitler's order. Smaller tables in a crescent arrangement were taken away. Post-war investigators found the receipt for this table, at 1,880. RM. The table was fabricated inside the Eagle's Nest as it wouldn't fit in the elevator.

7. Der Berghof Terrace. 1939. Bormann watches carefully over his boss' interaction with Eva Braun. Eva Braun had her own room at the Berghof, but Hitler did not want to appear too close or too friendly with her outside of tea-time

which was late at night by his fireplace. The stiff and unfriendly demeanor of the photo belies the truth. Bormann and Braun incidentally competed for visitation times to the Eagle's Nest when Hitler was away or in meetings.

8. <u>Hitler, Foreign Minister von Ribbentrop and French Ambassador F. Poncet</u>. Oct. 18, 1938. The moment is captured here when the first foreign diplomat stepped into the Eagle's Nest. There is an air of casualness among them. Poncet spoke fluent German and no interpreter was required, making it easy for Hitler to converse freely.

9. <u>Hitler and Eva Braun</u>. 1939. This photo was taken *in the Eagle's Nest*. This is the only picture in existence of Hitler showing any sort of affection for Eva Braun. Perhaps the isolation of the Eagle's Nest allowed Hitler to let his guard down. Often this photo is casted incorrectly in books as being taking in "Berchtesgaden," or "The Berghof."

10. <u>The Great Hall: Italian Princess Maria Jose</u>. Oct. 17, 1940. Here the princess' delegation sits to the left and Hitler's on the right. Hitler's group would experience different degrees of misadventure in life. To his right is Dr. Robert Ley, he hanged himself in his Nuremberg cell in 1945; Diplomat Walther Hewel, only 38 years old, was Hitler's trusted and well like liaison to von Ribbentrop. He shot himself in the head outside the Reich Chancellery on May 1, 1945; Adjutant to the Fuhrer, Wilhelm Bruckner, who seemingly leans back with indigestion met a weird end to his career: he got caught up in a scandal with the Berghof staff and was dismissed by Hitler after this luncheon; Reichsleiter Martin Bormann, half hidden, laughing, he flirts with Inge, the young, blond wife of Dr. Ley. She committed suicide in 1942.

11. The Great Hall. Hitler, Poncet (back to the camera), von Ribbentrop. Another angle of the first diplomatic meeting in the Eagle's Nest, Oct. 18, 1938. Notice the white vested, uniformed SS waiter looking out the window at the far side.

12. The Great Hall Fireplace. Oct. 23, 1938. This is one in a series of photos taken by Walther Hewel of the Goebbels' shotgun reconciliation. The Speers, Eva Braun and a few others joined in. Hitler seen here, is convincing Goebbels to do the right thing, as far as the Third Reich is concerned. The girl is Goebbels' daughter. There exists a lot of photos of Hitler and this girl together, there seems to be an affinity between the two, whether it is staged or not. Mrs. Goebbels murdered the child and her other children the day after Hitler killed himself.

13. Hitler on the Colonnade. 1939. There is a fantastic view of the Alps, a green valley and the Konig See from his vantage point.

14. The Great Hall, Hitler and Count Galazeo Ciano. Aug. 11, 1939. The handshake that sealed the deal. That is Italy would back Germany in an invasion of Poland. The next day Hitler would learn the Soviets would also sign a non-aggression pact between them at some point. The man in the middle, Col Nicholas von Below was Hitler's liaison man to Hermann Goring. Von Below was brought to this meeting to support Hitler's argument that the Luftwaffe would smash Poland and little resistance would be met. It was rare that Hitler brought military aides up to the Eagle's Nest. Von Below recalled Hitler telling him he liked to bring dignitaries up to the Eagle's Nest to "impress them."

15. Mercedes Leaving the Berghof for the Eagle's Nest. Aug 11, 1939. An interesting photo per the cult of personalities. Hitler sits in the front. Bormann's in the jump seat; Ciano and von Ribbentrop sit in the back. Typically Bormann did not ride with the diplomatic party as such; Albert Speer should be in this party but is left on the steps to go in the next car.

16. Princess Maria Jose. Oct.17, 1940. Hitler flicks his napkin, Bormann laughs and Maria Jose keeps her eye on both of them.

17. Dancing in the Eagle's Nest, June 3, 1944. Two nights before D-Day and the Nazis are whooping it up. Here they are celebrating the wedding of Gretl Braun to SS Obergruppenfuhrer Hermann Fegelein, Hitler's liaison man to Heinrich Himmler. Gretl is at left dancing with Hermann's brother Waldemar. Hermann Fegelein would be shot for desertion on April 29, 1945. He was executed in the Reich Chancellery garden. His brother Waldemar survived the war and lived until 2000 (aged 88). Gretl and Hermann did have a daughter (born after he was executed) whom Gretl named Eva, after her sister, Eva Braun. Eva Fegelein committed suicide in 1975 (aged 30) and her mother Gretl passed in 1987 (aged72).

18. The Allies Arrive at the Eagle's Nest. May 1945. Seemingly impressed with their conquest of the Fuhrer's secret hideout most GIs documented their visit. Getty Images.

19. 101st AB at Hitler's Round Table. 1945. The 101st were aggressive collectors of Third Reich objects in the Eagle's Nest. Over 35 watercolors of the Eagle's Nest rooms and exterior were found in the pavilion, they were initialed with "A.H." A GI shipped them Stateside.

20. 101ˢᵗ AB inside the Great Hall: The Fireplace. 1945. Getty Images.

21. Hitler on the Colonnade. July 1939. This photo occasionally appears in publications. Editors like to make it whimsical by stating "Hitler alone...contemplating...thinking what to do..." and so on. Actually on this July afternoon he is with his trusted inner circle of followers, including: Eva and Ilse Braun, Dr. and Mrs. Ley, Hitler's personal physician Dr. Morell and his wife, plus Goebbels', Bormann and adjutants who have not yet entered into the frame.

22. The Colonnade's New Owners. May 1945. New owners on Hitler's patio furniture. Getty Images.

23. The Great Hall: Gens. Eisenhower and Mark Clark, Sept. 2, 1945. When the area was cleared of SS snipers and Nazi fanatics Gen Eisenhower visited the ruins of the Obersalzberg. At around 3:30, after lighting a cigarette in Hitler's Great Hall Ike and Clark autographed Hitler's tea table. It was across this table Hitler had conversation with visiting diplomats about conquering Europe. Gen. John S.D. Eisenhower told me that Ike took down the "officers only" sign at the elevator to allow the enlisted to ride up instead of mountain climbing.

24. Gens. Eisenhower and Mark Clark Sign Hitler's Coffee Table. Sept. 2, 1945.

25. Sgt William Eckart rifle salutes Gens. Eisenhower and Mark Clark. 1945. The front MP is in Ike's personal security retinue, notice the finger on the trigger.

26. The Fuhrer on the Obersalzberg. 1939. From Heinrich Hoffman's photo album, U.S. National Archives.

27. <u>An Official State Silver Service Piece.</u> A cigar box with Hitler's state monogram, AH and an eagle clutching the swaz. There existed a total of 10 cigar boxes, 10 cigarette boxes and 10 tobacco boxes made by FDW of Munich.

28. <u>Berghof Terrace, Table with Cigar Humidor, 1939.</u> A silver humidor sits on the table to the lower left of Hitler who if fumbling with an unknown object. Its likely Hitler just sat down and the occupiers on the terrace have just left and were smoking. A valet will come by to collect the boxes to ensure no one lights up in front of the Fuhrer.

29. <u>Goirnghill, Residence of Hermann Goring.</u> 1939. Reichsmarschall Goring on the front terrace of his Obersalzberg house. His house actually faced the Berghof and a path existed from his door to the Berghof's driveway. The American's found over 10,000 bottles of wine and champagne in a marble lined cellar below the house, destroying them one by one.

# BIBLIOGRPAHY

Adams, Peter. Art of the Third Reich. Abrams, NY, 1992.

Below, Nicolaus von. Hitler At My Side, 1937-1945. Mainz, 1980.

Burckhardt, Carl. My Danzig Mission. Paris, 1961.

Ciano, Galeazzo. The Ciano Diary 1939-1943. Doubleday, 1946.

Eisenhower, Dwight D. Crusade in Europe, Heinenman, London, 1948.

Frank, Dr Bernhard. Hitler, Goring and the Obersalzberg. Plenk PG, 1989.

Galante and Silianoff. Voices from the Bunker. Doubleday, NY, 1989.

Gilbert, Martin, and Richard Gott. The Appeasers. London: St Martin, 1963.

Kershaw, Ian. Hitler 1936-1945. New York: Norton, 2000.

Hoffman, Heinrich. Hitler was his friend. London: Burke, 1955.

Irving, David. Goebbels: Mastermind of the Third Reich. London, 1966.

Payne, Robert. The Life and Death of Adolf Hitler. NY, 1973.

Playboy. Albert Speer Interview. June 1981.

Poncet, Francois. The Fateful Years. London, 1949.

Pope, Earnst. Munich Playground. New York: Putnam, 1941.

Price, Ward G. I Know these Dictators. London: Harrap, 1939.

Speer, Albert. Inside the Third Reich. New York: Macmillan, 1970.

Speer, Albert. Spandau: The Secret Diary. Phoenix, London, 1976.

Toland, John. Hitler. London 1977.

[1]  Speer. <u>Inside the Third Reich</u>
[2]  Frank. Hitler, Goring and the Obersalzberg.
[3]  Von Below. <u>At Hitler's Side</u>.
[4]  Poncet. <u>The Fateful Years</u>.
[5]  ibid
[6]  ibid
[7]  ibid
[8]  ibid
[9]  ibid
[10]  ibid
[11]  Speer. <u>Inside the Third Reich</u>.
[12]  ibid
[13]  Kershaw. <u>Hitler 1936-1945</u>.
[14]  ibid
[15]  ibid
[16]  ibid
[17]  Speer. <u>Inside the Third Reich</u>.
[18]  Ciano. <u>The Ciano Diary 1939-1943.</u>
[19]  Speer. <u>Inside the Third Reich</u>.